Re

by Cynthia Fenlon

HOUGHTON MIFFLIN HARCOURT
School Publishers

PHOTOGRAPHY CREDITS: Cover © Comstock/Corbis; 1 © Pixland/JupiterImages; 2 © B. Bird/Zefa/Corbis; 3 © Corbis; 4 © Pixland/JupiterImages; 5 © David R. Frazier Photolibrary/Alamy; 6 © David H. Wells/Corbis; 7 © Mel Yates/Getty Images; 8 © Denis Felix/Corbis; 9 © Comstock/Corbis; 10 © Getty Images/Blend Images

Printed in China

ISBN-13: 978-0-547-42720-1
ISBN-10: 0-547-42720-4

7 8 9 10 0940 18 17 16 15 14 13
4500396742

I can read
at the park.

I can read
at the beach.

I can read
at the store.

I can read
at the zoo.

I can read at a game.
I call out the score.

I **come** out in the yard.
I **hear** my mom read.

We go **away** in the car.
I hear my mom read.

I can read in bed.
I can read every day.

She **said** she likes
to read every day, too!

Responding

✔ **WORDS TO KNOW** **Word Builder**

Fill in the missing word in this sentence: I like to read _____ day.

✏ **Talk About It**

Text to Self Tell about a place you like to read every day.

WORDS TO KNOW

away	every
call	hear
come	said

TARGET STRATEGY **Summarize**

Stop to tell important ideas as you read.